THE
Uninvited Guest
And Other Jewish Holiday Tales

by NINA JAFFE

illustrated by ELIVIA

SCHOLASTIC
HARDCOVER

SCHOLASTIC INC.

New York

ACKNOWLEDGEMENTS

Many friends and colleagues helped to make the writing of this book possible. I would especially like to thank Howard Schwartz and Esther Hautzig, for all their support and encouragement, and Rabbis Rolando Matalon and Helene Ferris, for their advice and comments on several questions. I am indebted to Rabbi Michael Strassfeld, for reviewing and correcting the text for ritual detail and historical accuracy, and to the Jewish Theological Seminary, whose library staff allowed me such generous use of their collection and facilities.

Special thanks are due to my editor, Ann Reit; my agent, Carla Glasser; and to Ilise Benun, for her invaluable assistance. Above all, I wish to thank my husband Bob, who was there from the beginning.

Library of Congress Cataloging-in-Publication Data
Jaffe, Nina.
The uninvited guest and other Jewish holiday tales / by Nina Jaffe ; illustrated by Elivia Savadier.
p.   cm.
Includes bibliographical references.
Summary: Includes background information and retellings of traditional tales from Jewish folklore and legend related to major holidays, such as Yom Kippur, Sukkot, Hanukkah, and Purim.
1. Fasts and feasts — Judaism — Juvenile literature.   2. Jewish folk literature.   3. Legends, Jewish.
[1. Fasts and feasts — Judaism — Folklore.   2. Folklore, Jewish.]   I. Savadier, Elivia, ill.   II. Title.
BM690.J33   1993
296.4'3 — dc20   92-36308
CIP
AC

ISBN 0-590-44653-3

12 11 10 9 8 7 6   5 6 7 8/9

Printed in the U.S.A.   37

The illustrations in this book were done with Winsor Newton Brilliant Watercolors and Aquarelle Crayons, on rice paper, cotton canvas or Canson airbrush board.

First Scholastic printing, October 1993

Text design by Laurie McBarnette

For Louis, my son.
— N.J.

With love for my two precious Sadyes; Gay, Hayam and Lionel;
Janet, Emma, Ruth; Stanley, Dunya, and Margo; John
— and all our families.
— E.S.

CONTENTS

INTRODUCTION 7

ROSH HASHANAH — The Never-Ending Song 9

YOM KIPPUR — Miracles on the Sea
(Adapted from the story by I. L. Peretz) 17

SUKKOT — The Magician's Spell 23

HANUKKAH — Hannah the Joyful 32

PURIM — The Purim Trunk 41

PASSOVER — The Two Brothers 47

SHABBAT — The Uninvited Guest 55

ABOUT THE STORIES 62

ABOUT THE JEWISH CALENDAR 65

GLOSSARY 66

BIBLIOGRAPHY 71

RECOMMENDED TITLES 72

INTRODUCTION

The stories in this book are drawn from the folklore and legend that surround the holidays of the Jewish people. The holidays have been in existence, in varying forms, for more than three thousand years. Over the centuries, Jews have lived in many different lands, among many different cultures. Keeping the holiday traditions was one way of passing on a common Jewish heritage in every generation.

The holidays included in this book are: Rosh Hashanah, Yom Kippur, Sukkot, Hanukkah, Purim, and Passover. Shabbat, the weekly observance of the seventh day, has also been included. Each holiday has its own history, meaning, and customs, some of which are explained in the introductions to each story. From ancient times until today, telling holiday stories has enhanced the celebration of these special days. This collection was written for all children and their families to read, tell, and enjoy.

ROSH HASHANAH

Rosh Hashanah literally means "head of the year." It occurs on the first day of the Hebrew month called Tishri, in September or early October. On Rosh Hashanah many Jews go to synagogue to hear the *shofar,* the ram's horn, which calls the people to "wake up" and think about their actions during the past year. In ancient Israel, Tishri was also the time for bringing in the summer harvest, and plowing again for the winter. It was a natural time for the beginning of many activities.

In Jewish tradition, Rosh Hashanah is also a time to celebrate the creation of human beings and the beautiful, natural world that surrounds us. In fact, another name for Rosh Hashanah is *Yom Harat Olam,* "The day the world was created." The first story in this book, "The Never-Ending Song," is based on an ancient Jewish legend that tells of mythical beasts and the beginning of the world.

It is a custom on Rosh Hashanah to eat sweet things — apples dipped in honey, tasty holiday pastries, macaroons, or honey cake. Most of all, Rosh Hashanah is a time to reflect and to pray for a sweet New Year, a year of life, health, and peace for all living things.

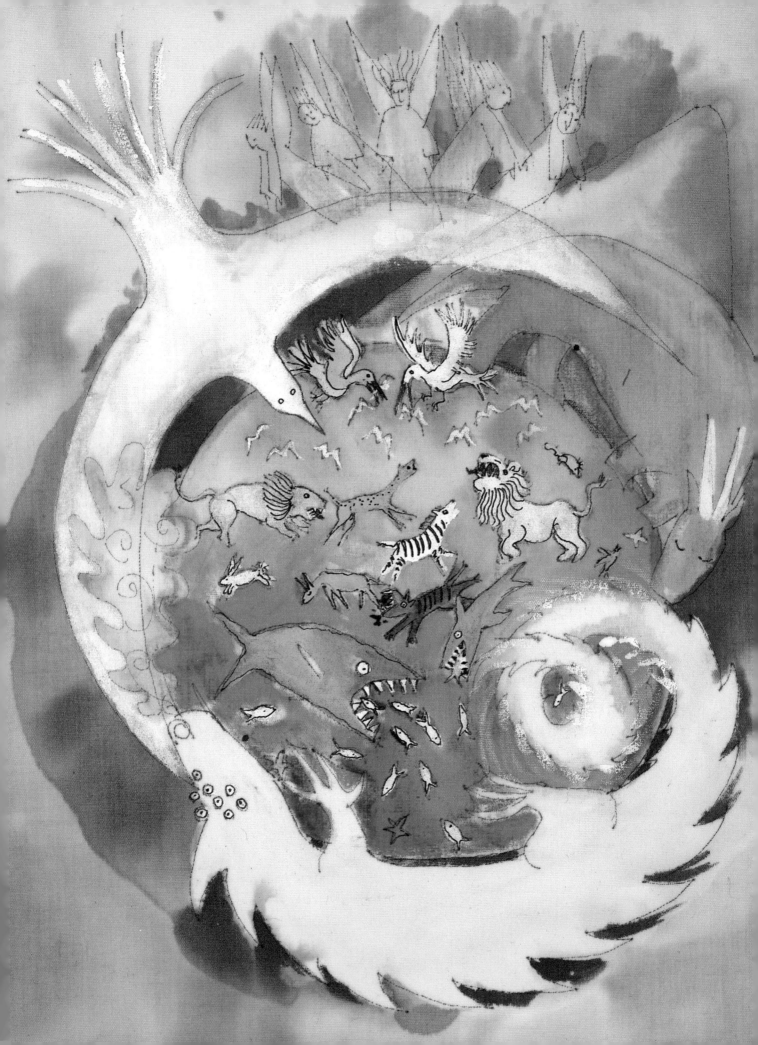

THE NEVER-ENDING SONG

Long, long ago, before the day human beings were created, all the creatures of the world were beginning to populate the earth and the sky. The greatest of all the birds was the Ziz. Her wings were as wide as the sky itself. When she stretched them out to fly, she could reach from one end of the earth to the other. It was the Ziz who, with her shining golden feathers, protected the earth from the hot winds of the south. Once, the egg of a Ziz broke and it flooded the forest and even the mountaintops!

Of the beasts of the field, the largest of all was Behemoth. His bones were as strong as brass. His legs were like great iron bars. He could drink the Jordan River with a single gulp and every day he grazed in the pastures of a magic mountain. When he finished eating in the evening, there was not a single blade of grass left to be seen, and yet, in the morning the meadows were lush and green again. His tail was as strong as a great cedar tree, and when he walked about, the earth trembled beneath him. Behemoth kept his home in a cave in the magic mountain, near the nesting place of his friend, the Ziz.

In the swirling waters of the sea lived the greatest sea monster of all time — Leviathan. He had as many eyes as the year has days, and scales that shone brighter than the sun itself. When Leviathan roamed the deep, one swish of his tail would cause huge tidal waves. Smoke poured from his nostrils and the water boiled and bubbled in his wake.

These were the great creatures of the sky and sea and earth, and they kept to themselves. At night, Leviathan would curl his tail around the ocean and sleep by the shores of the magic mountain, near his friends, Ziz and Behemoth, while up in the heavens, the angels sang them sweet lullabies.

But the Holy One had also put many other kinds of flying and creeping things in the world, large and small, and they were all trying to get used to their new homes. The small creatures were not having an easy time of it. The robins and sparrows were constantly being chased down by the great birds of prey — the eagles, hawks, owls, and condors. Day after day, they found that their nests had been robbed, and many of them were carried away by sharp talons, never to return.

The great sharks and barracudas never stopped feasting on the little fish. Wherever they turned, minnows and goldfish, guppies and trout were being hunted down in every corner of the ocean, in every lake, and in every river. On land, the lions and tigers, the great wolves and panthers were always at the heels of the mice and rabbits. The deer, the zebra, and the gentle giraffes never had a moment to rest from their running. In all the earth, there was no place to hide. The very world itself was being disturbed by the antics of small spirits and demons who ran about, hither and thither, turning mountains upside down and twisting the rivers out of shape.

Finally, all of the small creatures met to talk over their problems together. Something had to be done about this! Chittering and squawking, meowing and squeaking, they came to a spot that they all agreed might be safe, at least for a little while — by the roots of a great tree that stood near a gently flowing stream.

The rabbit spoke first. "We can't go on like this!" he cried. "There is no rest for me or my family. We are always running from some big animal!"

"You are right," croaked the frog. "Surely the Holy One did not create us to live like this!"

"We know that some of us must be eaten," chirped the sparrow. "After all, I myself must live on the bugs and insects. But if the hunting never stops, we will all disappear, and there will be no creatures left but the great beasts of prey!"

"You are right again," croaked the frog, "but what can we do?"

The animals, birds, and fish twittered and cheeped together for some time, but no one could come up with an idea. Finally, from the bottom of the stream, a little starfish made her way to the top. "Shhh," she whispered, "listen to me."

"Shhh," cried all the creatures. "Let us listen to the starfish."

And the starfish began: "My friends, I have been pushed by the currents of the water to many places on the earth. One day, a great wave washed me up on the shores of a shining beach. Near it stood a great mountain. I saw there three enormous creatures. None of you has ever seen creatures so great or so powerful, and as the sun went down, the angels sang them to sleep. Perhaps they could help us?"

The animals and birds agreed that each would send a representative to follow the starfish to the shores by the magic mountain. For what else could they do?

The mouse and sparrow followed the starfish as she made her way to the magic mountain. Just at sundown, Ziz and

Leviathan were about to take their rest (Behemoth had already gone into his cave), when they heard three tiny voices calling to them from the sandy shore.

"Please wake up, oh great creatures! It is only us, mouse, sparrow, and starfish, and we wish to speak with you."

Slowly, Leviathan uncurled his tail. Ziz fluttered and fluffed her wings, and Behemoth peeped out of his cave. "What do you wish, little ones?" they asked in one voice.

"Oh great ones, if you please," cried the mouse. "We have come to ask for help."

"Yes," said the starfish, "all over the world, the beasts and birds of prey and the hungry sharks stalk us little animals without cease. Spiteful demons are turning the mountains upside down. They are twisting the streams and rivers in all directions, just to confuse us. We are afraid that our kind will never have a chance to live in this beautiful world that the Holy One has created."

"That is why we have come," cheeped the sparrow. "Isn't there anything you can do?"

Leviathan blinked his hundreds of eyes. Behemoth sniffed into the winds and Ziz curled her mighty talons. For some time, they were silent. Then, they took counsel with the angels who were looking down from the starry heavens, and there was no sound of sweet lullabies that night. "It is time for the Great Words," they whispered among themselves.

"Yes," the angels agreed, "it is time."

Finally, they turned to the little ones and spoke again, in one voice. "Yes, little friends. There is something we can do. Return to your homes now, and wait."

The mouse, the sparrow, and the starfish hurried back to give the message to all their friends.

That year, in the month of Tammuz, when the air was hot and the summer sun burned down, Behemoth stepped out of his cave.

He lifted his great head and roared so loudly that the lions stopped in their tracks. His tail hit the ground with such force that the earth shook, and the tigers and wolves, the panthers and the jaguars trembled in their skins. They hid their heads in their paws and listened to the sound of the word as it entered their very hearts.

Out of their nests and burrows, the rabbits and mice popped their heads and, for the first time, breathed the breath of freedom as the stalking beasts rested from their ceaseless hunting.

The sound of that roar echoed on through the months of Av and Elul, until the autumn month of Tishri. Then the Ziz unfurled her enormous wings and uttered a cry that pierced through the very clouds of the sky. At the sound of that great cry, the eagles and hawks, the condors and the owls stopped in their flight, stunned and afraid. For the very first time, they felt pity and stopped their hunting for a time. They joined with the Ziz and called out her word in hoots and screeches until the winter month of Tevet.

Then, Leviathan raised his shining tusks from the depths of the sea. He whipped up the waves into a foaming froth that shook the barracudas and the swordfish from their path of destruction and hummed his word into the ears of the sharks and killer whales.

Out from behind the rocks and underwater crannies swam the little fish, lighting up the waters with flashes of silver, red, and gold. They listened as the big fish passed on the word through the currents of the oceans and streams as Shevat went by, and than Adar, until the gentle spring breezes of the month of Nisan blew in. In the heavens, the angels gathered their voices together and sang their word through the spheres until the demons bowed their heads in awe. The spirits put down the hills and mountains, and let the rivers follow their own course.

Ever since that time, the creatures of the earth have lived together, taking what they needed and no more, giving each other times of rest and play as well as times of hunting and fear. For the word of Behemoth was "Peace," and the word of the Ziz was "Justice." The word of Leviathan was "Mercy," and the word of the angels was "Love."

This is the ancient chant that circles the earth, that all animals, birds, and fish listen to and obey. Of course, all this happened before the time that human beings were created. But if you ever find yourself in a quiet place, in the woods or by the sea, and you listen very carefully, you too may hear the echoes of this never-ending song.

YOM KIPPUR

Yom Kippur, the Day of Atonement, is considered to be the holiest day of the Jewish year. It falls on the tenth day of Tishri (September/October) and signals the end of the High Holidays, which begin on Rosh Hashanah. On Yom Kippur there is no feasting or merrymaking. Yom Kippur is a day of fasting and contemplation.

In ancient Jerusalem, it was the one day of the year when the High Priest, dressed all in white, would enter the holy of holies, the innermost chamber of the Temple, to ask God to forgive the whole people of Israel for any wrong they might have committed in the past year. All the people would fast along with the priests. Later, a goat was chosen to be sent out into the wilderness. It was believed that the goat would carry the sins of the people far away, never to return. At sundown, the *shofar* was sounded for the last time. The people believed that if they had truly repented of their sins, God would bless them with life, peace, and health for the coming year, and inscribe them in the *Book of Life*.

In 70 C.E., the Roman Army destroyed the Temple in Jerusalem, and the Jewish people were flung to the far corners of the globe. To this day, it is a custom on Yom Kippur to fast and pray, and to listen to the last call of the *shofar*, as the old year ends, and the new year truly begins.

MIRACLES
ON THE SEA

Adapted from the story by I.L. Peretz

Long ago, in a foreign land, there lived a man named Satya. Satya was a fisherman, like his father and grandfather before him. He and his family lived in a small hut by the sea, far from the village, and every day Satya would go out to sea in his little wooden boat. Satya was a good fisherman. He knew all about the sea, and when the tides were coming in and out. He knew when the salmon would be running and when to watch the

sky for bad weather. He could guide his boat at night by looking at the stars. He knew how to patch his boat with tar and mend his nets. He even knew how to cut and clean his fish. Yes, when it came to the sea and fishing, there was no one as wise and experienced as Satya.

Like his parents and grandparents before him, Satya was also a Jew. But although he was wise in the ways of the sea, he knew little of the ways of his people. He didn't know how to sing the blessings for the Sabbath or how to make a Seder, or even how to say the letters of the Hebrew alphabet. And yet, there was one tradition that Satya and his family observed every year without fail.

On the afternoon before Yom Kippur, the holiest day of the year, Satya would take the biggest fish from his catch. Before sundown, he and his family would cook and eat part of the fish. All that night and through the next day, Satya and his family would fast. They would not eat or drink anything, not even water. And like all other Jews in their village, that one day of the year, they would dress in white, and go to the synagogue. Satya would sit and listen to the beautiful melodies of the Yom Kippur prayers. He was happy, even though he could not understand the words. At sundown, after the service was over, he and his family would return to their home. There they would break the fast and share the rest of the fish with their friends and neighbors. And so it went, always the same, year after year.

One year, in the fall, everyone in the village began to prepare for Yom Kippur as usual. On the afternoon before the holiday, Satya set out in his boat, for he had no fish in his nets that day. The sea was as calm as a sleeping baby, and the sky as clear as crystal glass. Yet all his friends had warned him, "Satya! Do not go out today! We're afraid the sea will become angry with a sudden storm!"

But Satya only laughed and said, "Look at the ocean. There is not a ripple, and the sky is blue. Besides, I can handle my boat in any weather!"

And so he set off. Satya rowed for a long time, but he had no luck. Every time he threw in his nets, they came up empty. Suddenly he saw before him a flash of light. It was a fish like none he'd ever seen before! A golden fish, with scales that glistened like the sun! Satya rowed faster and threw his net, but the fish dove under the boat and escaped. Again, a little farther ahead of him, the fish appeared. Satya threw out his net, but the fish dove through a wave and disappeared.

Satya chased the fish as it led him farther from the shore. Without realizing it, he was out of sight from land. Satya was growing tired, but he threw in his nets one last time. And just when it seemed he had finally caught the fish, the sky began to fill with heavy rainclouds. The waves rose all around him and the wind blew hard and strong, whistling past his ears. It took all of his strength to keep his little boat afloat.

Suddenly, Satya looked up. He saw that behind the wind and clouds, the sun was setting on the horizon. Yom Kippur is almost here, thought Satya to himself.

At that moment, he threw down his oars and crossed his arms over his chest, saying, "Come what may, I will not row on Yom Kippur!"

The waves lifted his little boat up like a matchbox and threw it down again. The wind whistled and shrieked, whipping the water into foam. Satya knew that his end might be near. But somehow he wasn't afraid. Instead, he began to hum the melodies he had heard so often in his little synagogue.

Satya sang, the wind howled, the waves pounded his boat. Surely, this is the end of me, he thought to himself, and closed his eyes in prayer. If he had kept his eyes open at that moment, he would have seen a strange sight. Out of the whirling mist, two figures appeared — an old man and an old woman, wrapped in flowing white robes, their faces glowing with a soft light.

They came near to Satya and whispered to him, "Sing, Satya, sing! Sing for Yom Kippur! The sea will hear you!"

As if in a dream, Satya sang louder and stronger. Slowly, slowly, the waves began to subside, and the wind died down.

"Sing for Yom Kippur, Satya!" they whispered again as they gently picked him up and lifted him above the water. High above the waves, they flew like birds with Satya in their arms until they laid him down on the sandy shore. Then, each one bent down and kissed him on the forehead as they spoke to him for the last time.

"*Shalom*, Satya, and may you be inscribed forever in the *Book of Life*."

Slowly, Satya opened his eyes. He looked around him, but no one was there. The sea was as calm as a sleeping baby. The sky was as clear as crystal, as the last rays of the sun peeped over the horizon. Satya rubbed his eyes. There was his little boat, rocking gently in the shallows.

"Surely this has all been a dream," he murmured to himself. But as he stood up to go, he saw a gleam of light thrashing in his nets. It was the golden fish.

Satya looked at the fish. Then he looked up at the sky. It seemed that the evening stars were smiling at him, so he smiled back. Then he picked up the fish and brought it home, ready to hear the Yom Kippur prayers and break the fast with his family and friends, as he did every year.

SUKKOT

In countries all over the world, the harvest is a time of festivity and thanksgiving. For Jews, the harvest holiday is called Sukkot, and it begins on the fifteenth day of Tishri (September/ October), although preparations for it start directly after Yom Kippur. The name Sukkot comes from the custom of building a *sukkah*, or "small booth," for the duration of the seven-day holiday. The sukkah needs to have at least three walls, made of any appropriate material, such as wood, or even cloth. But the roof must be made of branches cut from trees so that at night, anyone sitting in the sukkah can look out and see the stars. The sukkah is decorated with autumn fruits and vegetables, or any other craftwork the family or community wishes to add. Sukkot also commemorates the days when the Israelites wandered the desert, living in frail and fragile tents, in search of a new home.

In all countries where Jews have lived it is a tradition to say a blessing in the sukkah with the *lulav* and *etrog*. The etrog is a round, yellow citrus fruit that looks something like a lemon. It has a sweet pungent smell. The lulav is the branch of a palm tree, tied together with the branches of a myrtle and a willow tree. Together, these four plants are called "the four species," and they are very important to the celebration of Sukkot, for they represent four crops and the bounty of the harvest. "Shaking the lulav" during synagogue services is one of the most important observances of this joyous holiday.

THE
MAGICIAN'S
SPELL

Every year, the people in the small village of Masoret would celebrate Sukkot together. Every year, they would gather enough wood to build the walls of the sukkah. The children would go out to the fields and gather enough branches and harvest fruit to cover the roof and walls with sweet-smelling greenery. Every year, the rabbi would instruct the townspeople in the making of the lulav. He would show them how to weave together a palm branch with sprigs from myrtle and willow trees. From far off in the Holy Land, pungent etrog fruits had been sent across deserts and over seas and brought by wagons to the town square. Then, on the eve of Sukkot, all the families would enter the sukkah, to eat and pray together. The next day everyone gathered in the synagogue. The children would watch as the grown-ups said the special blessings and waved the lulav in all directions, shaking the branches as they marched in a grand procession.

For seven days and nights, the townspeople would take turns eating in the sukkah. At the end of the holiday, when the wooden·planks were pulled away, and the branches taken down, the children would say to each other sadly, "Now we have to wait a whole year till Sukkot comes again!"

One year, when the winds of autumn blew through the trees, a stranger came riding into town, pulling a brightly colored wagon behind him. It was the day before Sukkot, and the children had all gone out to the fields to collect branches and fruit. Only the grown-ups saw the stranger, as his horse clip-clopped down the cobblestone streets. Already, the carpenter had begun to put up the walls of the sukkah. The cooks and bakers were preparing delicious foods for the first meal of the holiday. In their homes, parents and grandparents were binding the branches for their lulavs, when they heard the stranger's call: "Herbs to sell! Cures for all ailments! Talismans and amulets for good luck and protection! Come buy my wares!"

On an ordinary day, if peddlers and traveling merchants passed through the village, the townspeople were always glad to sample their merchandise and hear their stories. The village of Masoret was high up in the mountains, and the folk who lived there did not often hear the news of the great goings-on in the valley below. But this day, no one stopped work to gather around the wagon. The carpenters kept up their hammering. The bakers kept up their mixing and kneading. The stranger called out again and again, but no one listened to him.

Finally, a tailor ran by the painted wagon, carrying a bundle of cloth in his arms, and said, "Sorry my friend. We have no time for traveling merchants today! The whole town is preparing for the holiday of Sukkot!"

When he heard these words, the stranger scowled. In every town where he stopped, the people would always crowd around his wagon, anxious to buy his potions and amulets (whether they worked or not). But in this town, no one had the time for him.

"Humph!" said the magician (for that, my friends, was the stranger's true profession). "So, they don't have time for me, eh! Building their house of leaves is more important than buying my precious merchandise! We'll see about that. I'll make sure that this town never celebrates this or any other holiday again, for forty generations!"

And with that, he entered his wagon, and took out a small, dusty red bag. He waved his hand over it three times, and spoke a few muttered words: "Magic Flowers of Forgetfulness, do my bidding! Let all who are now within the boundaries of these town walls forget their purpose. Erase the memory of this holiday from their minds and hearts! Let them go on as usual with their work and their lives, but let this and all celebrations be as a faded dream that once was known but is no more!"

With that, the magician stepped out of his wagon and emptied the contents of the bag into the wind. The autumn winds picked up the tiny flowers, which obeyed his command. The petals blew through every nook and cranny of the town. For a moment, the air was filled with a scent both strange and pleasing. The carpenter breathed it in, and put down his tools. The bakers smelled it and shut down their oven and boiling pots. The rabbi and cantor sniffed the air, and closed their holy books. In every house, the branches of the lulav were dropped to the ground and stepped on, unnoticed, by the parents and grandparents.

People got busy with ordinary things, and went back to their daily chores, as if nothing had ever happened. The magic flowers obeyed their master and then flew back, back to the wagon, and back inside the dusty red sack. The magician looked around him, satisfied that his spell had done its work. "Now let them try to celebrate! Let them try to remember anything more than their dull, empty lives! No one can withstand my powers, for I am the greatest magician of all time!" And with a triumphant cry, he whipped up his horse, and sped outside the village and down the road, to ply his wares in other lands, among other peoples.

Now, all this time, the children had been in the fields, gathering fruits and branches for the sukkah. The Flowers of Forgetfulness had not reached them, for all the while the magician was casting his spell, the children had been outside the walls of the town. When they returned to their homes, a strange sight met their eyes. The walls of the sukkah were half-standing, half-fallen down! Branches of palm trees, willows, and myrtle were scattered on the ground. Nowhere could they find a grown-up preparing for the holiday.

"Mother! Father!" they cried. "The sun is setting, we must finish the sukkah!" But their parents looked at them with wonder.

"Sukkah? What is a sukkah? What nonsense are you talking? Come in and wash your hands for dinner!"

The children gathered together and ran to the rabbi. "Rabbi, rabbi!" they called to him. "You must help our parents bind together the branches for the lulav!"

But the rabbi only shook his head. "What wild nonsense are you children chattering about? Go home to your parents. It's too late to be roaming about!"

The children gathered in the town square near the half-finished sukkah. Esther, one of the oldest girls, said, "Something strange has happened in our village. The grown-ups have forgotten Sukkot!"

Little David chirped up, "What can we do? We must do something to celebrate the holiday!"

Rebekkah picked up one of the fallen lulav branches, and slowly began to tie it to a myrtle twig. "I think I remember, watching my father. Didn't he wind a string around the branches, like this?"

"You're right," said Jonathan, "and look at those boards. I think I know how Simon the carpenter nails them together so they stand straight and tall."

One by one, the children cried to each other, "We remember! We know how to do it. Let's finish building the sukkah!"

The children hurried to their work. The oldest ones found hammers and nails. They put up the wooden planks till the four walls stood tall and straight. They climbed up ladders, and covered the roof with pine and evergreen branches. They decorated the walls with apples and pumpkins, colored cloth, and pictures they had drawn. The younger children gathered the fallen palm, myrtle, and willow branches. With their small fingers flying, they each set about to bind a lulav. Others went to find the etrogs that had arrived days before in their wooden boxes.

Finally, just before the sun was about to set, and the first evening star began to glimmer on the horizon, the children put down their tools. They folded up the ladders. They dusted off their hands. The sukkah was done! Everything was ready for the holiday. Tired from all their hard work, the children fell fast asleep in the sukkah they had built. All night long the stars twinkled down on them and shone through the branches on the roof.

In the morning, the children woke up and looked around at

each other. "Come on," said Rebekkah, "it's time to shake the lulav!" The children gathered around Rebekkah, as she held up her lulav and etrog. Carefully, they whispered the blessings and watched with round eyes as she waved the lulav to the front, to the right, to the back, to the left, upwards and downwards, shaking the branches in all directions. Then all the children followed her. The sukkah was filled with the sound of children's voices singing and waving their lulav branches.

Outside, the grown-ups had gathered. The magic flowers had made them forget, but they had not lost their curiosity. "What are the children doing in this peculiar little house?" they whispered to each other. "What funny games they are playing!"

At that instant a great clap of thunder burst through the sky. A fierce wind blew through the town, shaking the walls of the houses, scattering aside whatever lay in its path. The townspeople ran in fright, looking for shelter. Only the sukkah stood firm, with the children safe inside. From the heavens, rain began to fall in a drenching downpour. The rain came down in torrents, filling the gutters and flooding the narrow streets. Yet the sukkah remained dry and untouched.

Suddenly, just as quickly as it had begun, the rain stopped. How clean and clear the air smelled! And that strange yet pleasing scent that had lingered in the air for days was gone!

The townspeople came back to the square. They stood in front of the sukkah. The rabbi rubbed his eyes. The carpenter shook his head. The mothers and fathers, aunts and uncles, and grandparents blinked their eyes and wrinkled their noses.

"Rabbi," said the baker, "what are we doing outside the sukkah, while the children are all together inside?"

"Yes," said the carpenter, "who finished the walls of the

sukkah? The last thing I remember, I was just climbing the ladder to start the roof beams!"

"Children, children!" the grown-ups cried. "Let us in, it's time to celebrate Sukkot!"

Then the children knew that whatever evil spell that had been cast upon Masoret was broken. They ran outside and grabbed their parents and friends by the hands. "Come in, come in — we built it! Come in, it's time for Sukkot!"

At last, everyone was gathered together under the sweet-smelling evergreen branches. For the remaining days of the holiday, the people of Masoret ate in the sukkah, slept in the sukkah, laughed and talked and sang in the sukkah. And to this day, if you go to Masoret, you will see it is just the same; only the townspeople have made one small change in their tradition. Every year, when the winds of autumn blow, it is a child who nails the last board into the wall, and a child who places the last branch on the roof. And it is always a child who sings out the first blessing of the lulav — in remembrance of the time when the children saved Sukkot.

As for the magician, one day while casting his spell, he breathed in the flowers' scent himself, and forgot everything he knew. He lost his way in a dark forest, and was never seen again.

HANUKKAH

Hanukkah is a winter holiday that falls in Kislev, the ninth month in the Jewish calendar (November or December). Originally a minor festival, it has grown in importance through the centuries. The story of Hanukkah dates back in time to a period in Jewish history (roughly 175 B.C.E.), when Israel (then called Judea) was under the rule of Syrian-Greeks led by a king named Antiochus. Jews were forced to give up their religious beliefs and practices. Even the Temple in Jerusalem was taken over by the soldiers. Anyone daring to disobey these orders was put to death.

A small band of citizens, led by Mattathias and his five sons — Eleazar, Simon, John, Jonathan, and Judah — rebelled against Antiochus. They and their followers, who came to be known as the Maccabees, led a war of independence that finally ended in victory.

Legend has it that when the Maccabees returned to Jerusalem, only a small amount of oil remained to light the Temple's *menorah*. Miraculously, the tiny flame lasted for eight days, enough time for messengers to return with a full store of oil.

Hanukkah, then, is celebrated for eight days, in memory of this miracle. On each night, in homes and synagogues, another candle is added to an eight-branched *menorah* until, on the last night, all the candles have been lit. Hanukkah traditions are many and varied. Children play *dreidel,* a game of chance with a spinning top. Food cooked in oil, such as potato latkes or *sufganiyot,* is served. Gift-giving during Hanukkah is a more recent, North American development, but even in earlier times, children were given shiny coins, nuts, or candies. The story of the Maccabees, with its emphasis on religious freedom and its message of hope and faith, has made Hanukkah one of the most beloved celebrations of the Jewish year.

HANNAH
THE JOYFUL

Once, in a faraway land, there was a king who liked to disguise himself from time to time and walk among the people. "How else can I learn what my subjects are really thinking about," he reasoned, "and how they are living their lives?" Besides, he often found himself bored with life in the palace, signing royal documents day after day.

Now in this land, a Hebrew woman by the name of Hannah lived by herself in a small hut at the edge of the capital city. Hannah's parents had both died when she was very young, and so she had learned to fend for herself from an early age, as she had no other relatives to care for her. Yet all who knew her loved her for her good spirits. In the neighborhood where she lived, she was known as "Hannah the Joyful," for wherever she went, she brought a feeling of joy and gladness to share with each and every person she met.

One evening, in mid-December, the king decided to pay a visit to the Jewish quarter of the city. He knew that a winter holiday was being celebrated, and he wanted to learn more about it. Wrapped in a beggar's cloak, he

walked the chilly streets. As the sun set, he noticed many homes lit by menorah lamps. The smell of delicious holiday foods beckoned from the windows. Families were gathered together, singing and laughing. It was the first night of Hanukkah.

He continued on his way until finally he found himself at the far edge of town, standing at the side of a small house set back from a darkened, muddy side street.

Surely, he thought to himself, there can be no joyful celebrations in this miserable hut. Curious to see who lived there, he knocked on the door and called out as if he were begging for bread. Immediately, the door opened and Hannah welcomed in the stranger, for it was to her house that he had come.

The king was surprised by her hospitality, for he could see, despite the darkness inside, that her means were meager indeed, and she barely had enough to eat for her own holiday meal. Yet she invited him to sit down with her as she lit the first candle on the menorah, to share what little she had. He was surprised, too, at the happiness in her face, and the joy with which she sang the Hanukkah melodies.

"How do you earn your daily bread?" he asked. Hannah told him that she gathered salt from the waters of the sea, and sold it each day in the marketplace.

"How can you sing with such joy," he asked again, "when even tomorrow, you may not be sure of your next meal?"

"Tonight is the first night of Hanukkah, a night of joy, when we celebrate the miracle of light that was performed for our ancestors, the Maccabees, long ago. Even though I am alone, and an orphan, the Holy One has sustained me till now. For me, every day is a miracle. That is why I rejoice!"

"But what about tomorrow?" the king persisted. "How will you get on then?"

"Today is today. Tomorrow is yet to come!" replied Hannah as she bade the beggar farewell.

That night, as he returned to the palace, the king thought about what he had seen. He was impressed with Hannah's faith and trust in God. But would she remain steadfast and joyful in her praises, no matter what might befall her? The king wished to know the answer to this question, so he decided to put Hannah to a test.

The next day, the king sent a royal command throughout the marketplace: "It is forbidden to sell salt gathered from the sea, on pain of death!"

That evening, in his beggar's garments, the king went to visit Hannah. Once again, she welcomed him in. Once again, he saw her light the menorah, and sing with a joyful heart.

"Hannah, I was worried about you when I heard of the king's command," he said. "How did you find enough to buy a meal today?"

Hannah told him that by chance, as she stood in the marketplace, she had found an empty clay jar. "Just then," she said, "I heard a passerby say that he needed someone to bring water to his house. I ran to the well, filled my clay jar, and brought it home for him, in exchange for a few coins." So her daily bread had been earned.

"But what if things go wrong again?" he asked.

"Today is today," said Hannah, "a day of miracles. Tomorrow is yet to come. Come and sing with me!"

But the king departed. For he could not believe in her trust and faith.

The next day, the king sent forth a command, forbidding the carrying of water in clay jars, on pain of death. That evening he went to visit Hannah, and found her ready once again to share a simple meal, and to sing the praises of God as she lit the third candle. The king was amazed to learn that Hannah, on hearing of the royal ordinance, had joined a group of wood-cutters going out to the forest. She had gathered kindling along with them, and sold the wood in the marketplace.

And so three days passed. Each time the king threw an obstacle in her way, Hannah always found a new means to solve the problem and find her bread for the day. As the sun set, the king always found her at home, lighting the menorah and singing the holiday melodies with joy.

Now, it was a custom in this kingdom for all the citizens to take a turn serving in the royal guard of the palace. Man, woman, or youth, everyone was called to this special duty for one week out of the year. For that week, no salary was paid, but the guards were given a suit of armor and a steel sword to be kept for their time of service only. Anyone who disobeyed this order was considered a traitor and banished forthwith. When the new guards were called up for the week, the king made sure that Hannah's name was on the list. Surely now, without a way of earning even a day's wages, she will fall into despair, he thought to himself.

But to his amazement, on the seventh night of Hanukkah, when he appeared at her door, begging for his crust of bread, what did he see but Hannah, welcoming him in for a meal, and singing as usual! Upon asking her how she had accomplished this, she told this story, after he promised to repeat it to no one.

"Today I was drafted into the king's royal guard. I received no wages, but I did receive a beautiful steel sword. At the end of my rounds for the day, I went to the town wood-carver and sold it to him for a fair and reasonable price. In return, he was kind enough to carve me a wooden sword of the exact shape and size as the original. By the end of the week, I thought, I can find a way to buy the sword back, and the king's officers will never know the difference. As long as the swords are not inspected, no harm will come of it, for all day long I wear it by my side, in this leather sheath!"

The king now smiled to himself. For he was sure that he had trapped Hannah at last, and that he could throw an obstacle in her path that she could not overcome.

The next day, as Hannah was standing at her post, the grand vizier approached her and said, "A prisoner has been found guilty of thieving. You will be the executioner!" Hannah tried to protest, but what could she do? She was led to the courtyard of the palace. There was the poor prisoner, his head on the execution block as he knelt on the hard stones. Around about stood a crowd of onlookers, while the king himself stayed hidden behind the balcony pillars.

Hannah stood by the prisoner. She knew that she had to think quickly to save her own life as well as that of the prisoner — for had she not given away a sword of the king's guard? Hannah raised her voice and spoke to the crowd. "Oh my friends, know that I am a humble woman who obeys the laws of the Torah. I have never killed or hurt anyone in my life nor do I wish to. A prisoner has been accused of a crime. This is Kislev, the Hebrew month of miracles. As God came to the aid of my ancestors of old, I now beseech the Holy One to perform a miracle here, today!"

Hannah gripped the hilt of her sword and continued. "If this poor prisoner is guilty of a crime I will behead him as the law of the land requires. But if he is innocent, let this sword of steel turn to wood!'' And with that, Hannah drew the sword from its sheath.

The crowd gasped. Then they cheered. ''The sword has turned to wood! A miracle has happened! The prisoner is saved! The Lord has performed a Hanukkah miracle!'' Only the king knew the truth. And he realized now that Hannah would never lose her faith. Nor could she be outwitted!

That night, as she lit the eighth candle of her menorah, the king visited Hannah again. But this time he appeared at her door in his royal robes, revealing his true identity. With him were his counselors and the courtiers of the palace. ''This woman has taught me the true meaning of faith,'' he proclaimed. ''Let us honor her with joy and celebration!''

From that day on, Hannah and the king remained great friends. She advised him in many affairs of state, so that peace and happiness were soon spread far and wide, and all wars ceased. All the people of the kingdom soon grew to love and cherish her, and she was called ''Hannah the Joyful'' till the end of her days.

PURIM

"On Purim, everything is possible."
"After a Purim meal, not even a dog goes hungry."
"When Purim comes, one forgets all problems."

These are only a few of the Jewish folk sayings about this wonderful holiday. Purim, which falls on the 14th of Adar (generally in March), is similar to the carnival festivals that take place in many countries at this time of year.

In Jewish tradition, this annual event is celebrated with the reading of the *Megillah*, or scroll, of Esther, one of the later stories to be included in the Bible. The *Megillah* tells of a wicked plot by an evil minister, Haman, to destroy all the Jews of Persia. Eventually, the Jews are saved through the cleverness of the king's new wife, Esther, and her cousin, Mordecai. At the end of the story, Haman is killed and the Jews turn defeat to victory through armed combat. According to the story, Haman drew lots to pick the day for the destruction of the Jews, and it was on that same day that they saved themselves — the 14th of Adar.

On Purim, people disguise themselves as the characters in the story, or in any costume that pleases them. In the synagogue, during the reading of the *Megillah*, children use noisemakers to drown out Haman's name every time it is read in the story. In some Jewish communities a Purim feast is held and gifts of food are sent from household to household, including *hamantaschen* cookies, sweets, and fruit. For young and old, Purim is a time for jokes, lively antics, and merry-making. These are a few of the reasons why Purim has been a favorite Jewish holiday for generations.

THE PURIM
TRUNK

Once upon a time in the town of Chelm, there lived an old melamed, a Hebrew teacher named Yankel, and his wife, named Reshka. They were very, very poor, and lived in a little house right on top of a hill, on the same street as the synagogue. One night, just after Hanukkah was over, the two of them were sitting in the kitchen by the stove to keep warm, when Yankel began to sigh a big sigh. "Oh, Reshka, Purim is coming soon, but we don't have enough money for hamantaschen. Just once I'd like to eat a nice, sweet, poppyseed hamantasch for Purim!"

And Reshka said, "Oh, Yankel, you are right. I too would love to have hamantaschen for Purim, but where will we get the money to pay for it?"

Suddenly, Yankel had an idea. "I know what," he said. "You know that old trunk that was given to you as a dowry? The one with the wheels on it that we keep in the attic? Let's bring it down, and once a week you will put in a coin, then I will put in a coin, and by the time Purim comes around, we'll have saved enough money for . . . HAMANTASCHEN!"

The first week everything went just as they had planned. Yankel put in his coin, and Reshka put in her coin. But the next week, Yankel thought to himself, "Why should I put in a coin? My salary is small enough as it is! Let Reshka put in her share. She has saved more than enough."

And when it came to Reshka's turn, she thought to herself, "Why should I put in even a *groschen*? I barely have enough to pay the bills as it is! Let Yankel put his own coins in!"

And so it went, week after week, and neither of them knew what the other was up to.

It was the day before Purim. Yankel said, "It's time to open up our trunk." Slowly, they lifted the lid and when they looked inside, Yankel cried, "Nothing! It's empty! Somebody has stolen our savings!"

"A thief has been in our house!" shrieked Reshka. All of a sudden, she looked at Yankel and said, "Did you put your coin in every week, as we agreed?"

And Yankel looked at her and said, "No, why should I? Didn't you put in yours?"

Reshka shook her head. As soon as he realized what had happened, Yankel began to yell at his wife. "Woman of evil! A thousand curses on your head! Now we have no money for hamantaschen!"

And she began to scream, "You foolish man! May you dream of spiders crawling in your bed and never wake up! You've ruined everything!"

They began to fight. Yankel grabbed Reshka's wig and tried to pull it off. Reshka grabbed on to Yankel's beard. Back and forth they went, pulling and grabbing, shrieking and yelling, when all at once they both fell into the trunk, the lid snapped shut and, with the two of them still fighting inside, the trunk began to move.

Since Yankel and Reshka were so poor, they had no threshold built into their doorway. And so the trunk rolled right through the door. And since they lived at the top of the hill, the trunk

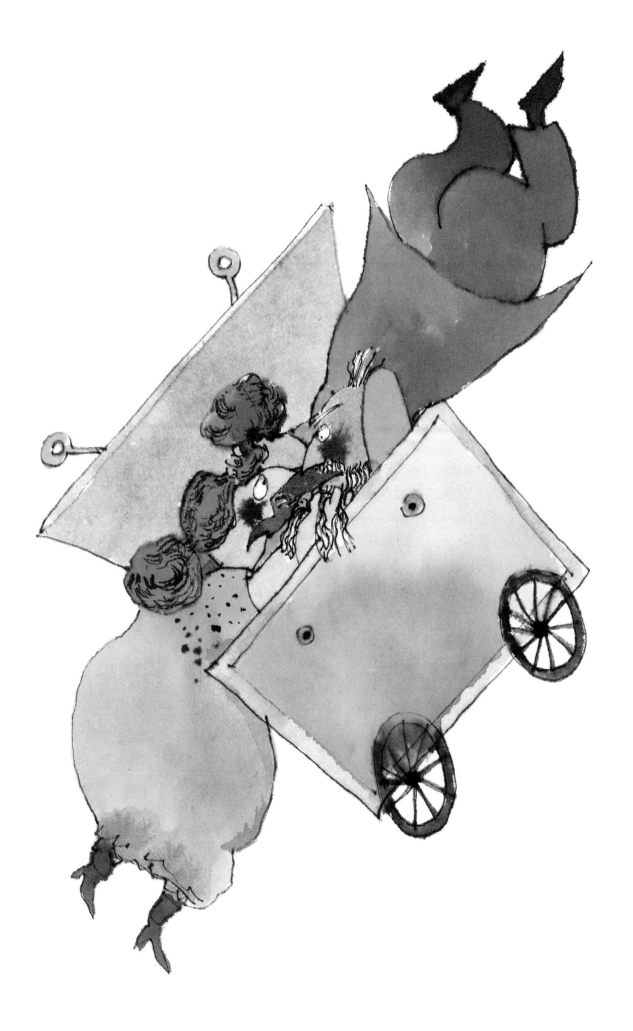

rolled down the street. Down and down it went, with the most terrible shrieks and unearthly noises coming from inside, until it stopped right in front of the synagogue.

The people of Chelm were terrified. They all gathered around. What could it be? Surely this trunk was possessed by devils or demons, or maybe even the ghost of Haman himself! They realized there was nothing to do but open the trunk and find out for themselves. The rabbi stepped forward. Everyone began to pray as he snapped open the lock. Slowly, he opened the lid and declared, "Yankel the melamed and his wife Reshka!" She was still grabbing at his beard and he was still trying to pull off her wig.

When the people of Chelm heard their story, they sent Yankel and Reshka home with a basket of hamantaschen for each. But they wanted to make sure that nothing like this ever happened again in the town of Chelm. Their wise men sat and argued, and after seven days and seven nights, they called all the people together in the town square and read them the new laws that had been decreed for all the people of Chelm to obey from that day onward:

One — No melamed could ever again live on the same street as the synagogue.

Two — Every door in Chelm must have a threshold.

Three — Never again in Chelm could a trunk be built with wheels!

PASSOVER

The Passover Seder is the festive meal that commemorates what was perhaps the most powerful event in the shaping of the Jewish people — the Exodus from Egypt. Passover (or *Pesach*, as it is called in Hebrew) comes in the spring, on the fifteenth of Nisan, the first month of the Jewish year (usually in April). It is also known as the Festival of Freedom, and the Feast of Unleavened Bread.

During the Seder, the story of the Exodus is recounted from an age-old book called the *Haggadah*. This story tells how the ancient Israelites were led out of slavery in Egypt by the prophet Moses. It is told that God performed many miracles to convince Pharaoh, the ruler of Egypt, to let the Israelites go. In their flight, God parted the waters of the Red Sea so that Moses and his people could cross safely to dry land, and a free way of life. In the *Haggadah*, the presence of symbolic foods, such as *matzah* (unleavened bread) and bitter herbs, is explained. Songs are sung and children are given a prominent role in the service. In Arab lands such as Morocco, it was a custom for members of the Jewish community to go from house to house reenacting events of the story.

At the end of every Seder, the door is opened to the legendary figure of the prophet Elijah, messenger of hope and peace, who is welcomed as an honored guest, and even offered his own cup of wine. Hospitality and sharing with others are important themes of the celebration of Passover.

do you bother me with your troubles? Take yourself and your problems and go to *Azazel!*" Azazel is a Hebrew word for a far-away place, a wilderness where demons are said to dwell. Yacoub had told his brother to go to the devil!

What could poor Yousef do? He went home, and there were his wife and children, crying from cold and hunger. So he packed up his tallit and tefillin, slung the bag over his shoulders, and said to them, "Do not cry, children. If God is good to me, I'll be home again in time for our Seder." And he set off to look for Azazel.

He walked and walked all day under the hot sun until he came to a stream. There he ate a bit of crusty bread, said his evening prayers, and went fast asleep. In the morning he woke up, washed his hands, said the morning blessings, and once again went on his way.

He continued on until he came to a little house by the side of the road. Perhaps this is the place of Azazel, he said to himself.

He knocked on the door and went inside, but all he saw there were three young women, sitting and spinning. One was spinning woolen thread. The next was spinning silver thread. And the third was spinning golden thread. They welcomed him in and gave him food and drink, but he noticed that they all looked very sad. When he asked them why, they began to cry.

"We are sad because we are waiting for our fiancés, but they never come, so we must sit all day and spin. That is why we are crying."

Yousef said, "Do not worry. If God is good to me and my way prospers, I will find out why your fiancés never come."

The three spinners thanked him and gave him more food and drink for his journey.

He went on until he came to a tall and beautiful fruit tree. He reached up, picked some fruit, and began to eat, but as soon as he tasted it, he cried out, "Ugh! This fruit tastes bitter!" And he threw it away.

"Oh tree, why is your fruit so bitter?" he asked.

"I wish I knew," sighed the tree. "For every time a traveler passes this way and tastes some, they give me a curse instead of a blessing!"

"Do not worry," said Yousef, "for if God is good to me and my way prospers, I will find out why."

The tree thanked him and he went on until he came to a deep river. The only way to get across was in a boat, rowed by a ferryman who cried like a child. When Yousef asked him why he wept, the ferryman replied, "Day after day, year after year, I take people back and forth across the river, but I myself can never leave the boat! That is why I weep!"

And Yosef replied, "Do not worry, my friend. For if God is good to me, I will find a way to help you!"

The ferryman thanked him and set him down on the other side of the river.

Now Yousef found himelf in a deep, dark forest. He followed a narrow path through the trees until he came to a tiny hut. He did not know it, but he had reached the home of the wise woman in the woods, the woman who knows the answers to all questions. After giving him supper, the wise woman said to him, "Do you have a problem? How can I help you?"

Yousef knew exactly what he wanted to say. "Why do the bridegrooms of those three maidens who sit and spin never come?"

And the wise woman answered, "That is because they never

sweep the fallen leaves from in front of their door. If they swept away the leaves, their fiancés would come."

"And why is the fruit of that tree so bitter?" he asked again.

"The fruit is bitter because there is a treasure hidden beneath its roots. If someone were to come and dig up the treasure, the fruit would become sweet again."

"And why can the ferryman never leave his boat?"

"Oh well, if someone were to come and take his place, then he could go!"

"And why," said Yousef, "has my brother hardened his heart against me?"

"That is because he himself has never known what it is to be hungry."

"And when can a poor man ever find happiness?"

"When he finds what he has given up for lost."

Now Yousef was ready to ask his last question, "Oh wise woman — for surely you must be the wise woman of the woods — can you tell me, where can a Jew find matzah, who has none?"

"Let him take from one and give to the other," she replied.

Now Yousef was happy, for he had all the answers to his questions. He started off for home. When he came to the river, he told the ferryman what the wise woman had said: "If someone were to come and take your place, you would be free to go!"

The ferryman was overjoyed, and gave him many gifts to take home to his family.

When he reached the tree, he said, "Oh tree, there is a treasure buried under your roots, but if someone were to take it away, your fruit would become sweet again!" At that very instant, a hole opened in the ground, and in it, there was gold and silver and diamonds! Yousef filled his pockets and when he was through, the ground closed up again, as if nothing had been there.

"Oh, thank you, thank you!" said the tree as it showered him with its new, sweet fruit to take home.

When he reached the three maidens spinning, he told them what the wise woman had said: "If you sweep the leaves away from the front door, your bridegrooms will come!"

The young women thanked him, and each gave him a gift. The first maiden gave him a ball of woolen thread. The second one gave him a ball of silver thread, and the third one gave him a ball of golden thread.

Now Yousef hurried home, and with his new-found wealth, he and his wife and children were able to have a beautiful Seder, with a snow-white tablecloth, golden candlesticks, and the most delicious food, wine, and matzah!

Naturally, they invited all their friends and family to join them. When Yacoub entered the house, his face turned green with envy.

"Where has all this wealth come from?" he asked.

"Brother, don't you remember? When I came to your house asking for wheat, you sent me to Azazel. I have brought all these things from Azazel."

That night, Yacoub could hardly sleep, thinking of the treasures he would find. Before the sun rose, he awoke and hurried down the road to find Azazel. When he reached the river, he jumped into the boat and said to the ferryman, "Take me to Azazel!"

Immediately, the ferryman understood what he had to do.

"We are almost there," he said, "but you must take the oars and row the rest of the way."

Yacoub reached over and grabbed the oars, but as soon as they reached the other side, the ferryman jumped out, and went running down the road, for now he was free!

Ever since then, Yacoub, who cared for no one, has been sitting in that boat, rowing people from one side of the river to the other. Day after day, year after year.

He wanted to send his brother to Azazel, but he ended up there himself!

SHABBAT

Shabbat, meaning "Sabbath," is not a holiday that happens once a year. It is a holy day that occurs every week. Shabbat is so central to Jewish tradition that hundreds of songs and poems have been written about it, and it has its own special store of legends and tales. In the *Torah,* keeping Shabbat is one of the Ten Commandments: "Remember the Sabbath day and keep it holy. Six days you shall work, but the seventh day is a Sabbath unto the Lord."

In Rabbinic legends, the Sabbath, along with the Torah, was considered to be in existence before the world was created. On the Sabbath it was ordained that men, women, children, and even animals were to rest, just as God rested on the seventh day after the work of creation.

Shabbat begins on Friday evening, at sunset. In many Jewish homes, family members gather together to say blessings over the wine and the *challah* before sitting down together to enjoy their meal, and the following day of rest and prayer.

One image found in many of the songs and stories about Shabbat is that of the Sabbath as a Queen. A famous Hebrew verse, "L'chah dodi," written in the sixteenth century, is still recited on Friday evenings in synagogue. The poem says: "Come, my friend, let us greet the bride, let us welcome the Sabbath Queen into our home."

In story after story, Jewish tales around the world reflect a belief in the almost magical powers of Shabbat to bring forth blessings of peace, good fortune, and well-being.

THE UNINVITED
GUEST

Once, there lived a young couple named Sarah and Avram. Avram was a peddler. Six days a week he would travel on foot from town to town, selling his wares. Sarah stayed home and looked after their little cottage. On market days, she would go into town and sell vegetables from their garden. But on Friday afternoon, no matter how far he had traveled, no matter how little he had sold, Avram always made his way home, so that he and Sarah could be together to celebrate the Sabbath.

As the sun went down, Sarah would recite the blessing and kindle the Sabbath candles. Together, they would welcome the spirit of the Sabbath — the Sabbath Queen — into their humble home, singing, "Come, my friend, let us greet the bride, let us welcome the Sabbath Queen into our home." In the glowing light, they would bless each other in the words of the ancient priests, "May God bless and keep you. May He watch over you in kindness. May He grant you a life of good health, joy, and peace." Only then would Avram recite the Kiddush over the wine, recalling the Seventh Day and the Creation of the World and the People of Israel. Only then would they break open the sweet and warm challah loaves that Sarah had baked, joining hands across the wooden table. Smiling at each other, they knew that no matter how hard life might be, they would always have this holy day to share for all their years together.

Time passed. Avram continued to peddle his wares. Sarah continued to care for their home and garden. In the evenings, when Avram was away, she would sit alone, or with a friend, sewing a quilt or wall-hanging, telling stories or reading in Yiddish in the holy prayerbook. The couple had no children, but still they rejoiced in their love for each other, in the time that they shared together. And often on a Friday afternoon, Sarah would see Avram walking down the road with a friend, or some poor stranger who had nowhere to go for the Sabbath. "We may be poor," they would say to each other, "but we always have enough to welcome travelers or people in need to our home. There is always enough flour for the challah. There are always enough coins to buy the wine and the candles. We always have enough to welcome the Sabbath Queen to our home. We may not have children, but our lives are full — for we are blessed with the mitzvot that God has enabled us to perform!"

One year, the winter was colder than usual. A heavy snow had fallen, and for weeks the roads were covered with high drifts. Then the snow melted, and the mud made the roads impassable. It was hard for Avram to go on his usual rounds. Sarah too, could not make her way to the marketplace. Little by little, the money they had saved for hard times had to be spent, until one week, they had almost nothing left. Finally, the roads began to dry. A warm and gentle spring sunlight began to shine on the frozen hills and valleys, and one day, old Avram threw his sack on his shoulder and set off to earn what he could for the week.

Sarah bent over their patch of land and began to weed and hoe for the spring planting. On Friday morning, she set off for town to buy what little she could with their last coin. On the way, she met the town melamed, the schoolteacher. He stopped her and said, "Good morning, *Froy* Sarah. Over the winter, many of our books were damaged by the cold and melting frost. Could you give something for their repair?" Without a moment's hesitation, Sarah dropped her last coin into the melamed's outstretched hand — for what could be more important than the learning of children? The study of holy books?

Then she turned and made her way home. Surely, she thought to herself, there will be enough at home for our Sabbath meal. But when Sarah reached home, there was little to be found. She searched in every corner. High up in the cupboard, she found an old bottle of wine, and two white candles. But search though she might, she could not find a speck of flour anywhere in the house. Soon Avram would be coming home, and there would be no challah in the house for the Sabbath! Never before had such a thing happened to them. Sarah thought of running to a neighbor, but it was too late. In all the time she had spent in her search, the sun had been going down! Now it was almost sunset. In the waning light, she saw Avram coming up the road, and with him was a guest! He must have met some poor traveler on his way, and now, she had nothing to offer them. No food had been prepared, and there was no challah!

Quickly, Sarah set the table for three. She set the candlesticks in the middle, along with the Kiddush cup and the bottle of wine. The challah plate sat on the table. Oh, how empty it looked! Sarah said a quick prayer to herself. "Somehow," she whispered, "God will provide." Right outside the doorway, she spied two round stones. In a flash, Sarah picked them up and put them on the challah plate, covering them with the embroidered cloth they always used. At least when Avram and their guest entered, it would feel like the Sabbath!

Avram opened the door. With him was an old woman, her head covered with a broad kerchief. "See Saraleh, this poor woman was lost on the road. I have brought her here to spend the Sabbath with us." Sarah could not speak. She could not bring herself to tell Avram the truth: that their one pride and joy, their lovely Sabbath ceremony, would be flawed and lacking. She closed her eyes and recited the blessing over the candles. They sang the ancient prayers to each other and welcomed in the Sabbath Queen. Avram recited the Kiddush. All the while, their guest, the old woman, sat with her head down, not speaking a word, only whispering "Amen" after each blessing.

Then Avram reached out his hand to uncover the challah loaves. Filled with shame, Sarah put one hand over her mouth and reached out to stop him. "No Avram! They are only — " when, quick as the wind, the old woman lifted off the cover herself. And there, on the plate, sat two golden, sweet-smelling loaves of challah, warm and shining on the table.

Sarah stammered, "But, they were only stones, just a moment ago!"

The old woman let her kerchief fall. As she raised her eyes, she seemed to grow taller and younger. Avram and Sarah stared at her in awe. Her hair shone brighter than the light from any candles, and a garland of flowers wreathed her head. It was the bride of the Sabbath, the Sabbath Queen herself, who had come to visit them!

She spoke to them, and her voice was sweet as a nightingale's singing in the morning. "How often have you welcomed me into your house, with joy and gladness. Each Sabbath, you bless each other and the Creator of the World with love and peace in your hearts. How often have I longed to reward your faithfulness, and your kindness to others. Now I have a blessing for you — May the Holy One watch over you both and keep you well, to perform the Holy Mitzvot, the Sacred Commandments. And when your days on earth have ended, may you celebrate the Sabbath, together with the angels, in the Garden of Paradise, for all time to come." And with that, she touched their bowed heads, waved her hands once over the candles, and vanished into the spring night.

Avram and Sarah clasped their hands together. As they stood across from each other, gazing at one another in wonder, it seemed that the light of a thousand stars shone in each other's eyes, and the laughter of a thousand children filled the room.

ABOUT THE STORIES

ROSH HASHANAH — THE NEVER-ENDING SONG

"The Never-Ending Song" is adapted from the *Midrash* (a Hebrew word that means, literally, "to draw out"). Midrashim are stories, parables, and legends told by the rabbis of old in order to explain, or elaborate on, passages from the Torah. In this story, you read of mythical beasts and monsters named Ziz, Behemoth, and Leviathan. The origin of these names goes back to ancient times. The Jews of the Near East were influenced by the mythology and cultures of the people who surrounded them, such as the Egyptians, Babylonians, and Canaanites. These mythic images found their way into the stories and writings of the ancient Hebrews, and became incorporated into lore and legend, taking on their own unique significance in Jewish culture. Mention of these creatures can be found in the Book of Genesis, Psalms, the Book of Job, and other texts dating back to the first century.

Source: *Legends of the Bible* by Louis A. Ginzberg

YOM KIPPUR — MIRACLES ON THE SEA

The original version of "Miracles on the Sea" was written by the Yiddish writer, Isaac Loeb Peretz. Yiddish was the language spoken by the vast majority of the Jews of Eastern Europe. Although millions of Yiddish-speaking Jews perished in the Holocaust, the language can still be heard in small Jewish communities throughout the world, and in Israel. Today, there are still newspapers, books, and magazines being published in Yiddish.

In the late nineteenth and early twentieth centuries, a group of young Jewish writers decided that it was time to write stories and novels in Yiddish, just as there were works of literature in many other European languages. One of the greatest of these writers was I.L. Peretz. Born in Poland, and steeped in his people's traditions, Peretz captures in his writing the essence of the Eastern European Jewish experience with pathos, humor, irony, and imagination. Today, the writings of Peretz have been translated into many other languages so that we can enjoy him now, as much as his first readers did at the turn of the century.

Source: I first encountered this story in *The Case Against the Wind and Other Stories by I.L. Peretz,* translated and adapted by Esther Hautzig.

SUKKOT — THE MAGICIAN'S SPELL

This is an original story inspired by folkloric themes. The name of the fictional town, Masoret, is a Hebrew word meaning "tradition."

HANUKKAH — HANNAH THE JOYFUL

There are many Jewish folktales that take place during the holiday of Hanukkah. Often they focus on the power of faith and tell of miracles occurring on behalf of a needy but deserving person, male or female. A strong theme, not only in Jewish but in all folk traditions, is that of a poor but clever protagonist who uses both wits and faith to overcome obstacles. In most cases, the hero or heroine of the story is rewarded, and often elevated to a higher social position.

Source: "Blessed Be God, Day by Day" in *Folktales of Israel* by director of the Israel Folktale Archives, Professor Dov Noy, as recorded from an Afghani immigrant to Israel. Another version of this story can be found in Howard Schwartz's collection, *Elijah's Violin and Other Jewish Fairy Tales,* under the title, "The Wooden Sword."

PURIM — THE PURIM TRUNK

"The Purim Trunk" takes place in a town called Chelm. Chelm was a real town in Poland. But in Jewish folklore, it is more famous as an imaginary village where the townspeople and their rabbis are constantly undoing themselves through foolish actions and backward thinking. Chelm is an upside down sort of place all year around, where people try to capture the moon in a barrel, or plant salt in the ground when they are running out of it. Chelm stories present some of the most beloved characters in all of Jewish folklore, and they are perfect companions to the holiday of Purim.

Source: An earlier rendition of this story can be found in *A Treasury of Jewish Folklore* by Nathan Ausubel, and other collections of Jewish folklore.

PASSOVER — THE TWO BROTHERS

The story of a selfish or greedy sibling receiving just deserts can be found in countless folktales worldwide. This particular story is a favorite of mine for telling at Passover and other times of the year. Yacoub and Yousef are familiar names in Arabic and Judeo-Arabic cultures.

Source: "Where Is the Place of Azazel?" in *Moroccan Jewish Folktales,* collected and edited by Professor Dov Noy, Director of the Israel Folktale Archives in Jerusalem

SHABBAT — THE UNINVITED GUEST

The motif of a stone being turned into a challah by a mysterious guest can be found in Jewish folktales as well as in more contemporary stories, including "Revealed," also by I.L. Peretz, translated by Esther Hautzig in *The Case Against the Wind.*

ABOUT THE JEWISH CALENDAR

This book introduces you to many of the names for the Hebrew months. These names, dating back to Babylonian times (approximately sixth century B.C.E.), had particular meanings, many of which are lost today. But we do know, for example, that *Tammuz,* the summer month, means "fruitfulness" and that *Tishri,* the seventh month, means "opening of the year."

The Hebrew months roughly approximate the Western, or Gregorian, calendar in the following manner:

Nisan (nee-SAHN)	March–April
Iyyar (ee-YAHR)	April–May
Sivan (see-VAHN)	May–June
Tammuz (tah-MOOZ)	June–July
Av (ahv)	July–August
Elul (eh-LOOL)	August–September
Tishri (TEESH-ree)	September–October
Cheshvan (chesh-VAHN)	October–November
Kislev (KEES-lehv)	November–December
Tevet (TEH-veht)	December–January
Shevat (shuh-VAHT)	January–February
Adar (ah-DAHR)	February–March

Among the Jewish holidays not included in this book are: *Shavuot,* "The Giving of the Ten Commandents"; *Simchat Torah,* "Rejoicing in the Torah"; *Tu B'Shevat,* "The New Year of Trees"; *L'ag Ba'Omer,* "The Scholar's Holiday"; Israel Independence Day; and *Yom Ha Shoah,* "Holocaust Remembrance Day."

GLOSSARY

Many of the words in this book come from other languages, such as Hebrew or Yiddish. Sometimes, even in English, these words are pronounced differently depending on who is speaking and where they come from. The following guide will help you to pronounce the words that may not be familiar to you. Enjoy trying out these new sounds!

Note: "Ch" in Hebrew is pronounced like the ending sound of the English expression *"Yech!!"* You can try it out when you read words like "challah" or "schach." An (H) after a word means it is from Hebrew. A (Y) means that it is from Yiddish.

Azazel (ah-zah-ZEHL) (H): In Jewish legend, a wilderness where demons were said to dwell.

B.C.E.: Before Common Era is equivalent to B.C.

Book of Life: It is a traditional belief that, on Rosh Hashanah, as past actions are being accounted for, the names of all righteous and worthy people are written in the *Book of Life. L'shanah tovah tikatevu,* meaning, "May you be inscribed for a good year [in the *Book of Life*]," is a common greeting during the High Holidays.

C.E.: Common Era is equivalent to A.D.

Challah (HAH-lah) (H): The braided loaf of bread over which a blessing is said at the Friday evening meal. Two loaves are placed on the challah plate, as a reminder of the extra portion of manna that God provided for the Israelites as they wandered in the desert, as told in the Book of Exodus. On Rosh Hashanah, a round loaf is used to symbolize the wish for a round, *whole* year.

Dreidel (DRAY-del; rhymes with "cradle") (Y): It is a custom at Hanukkah to play a game with this spinning top. The letters on the dreidel — *Nun, Gimel, Hay,* and *Shin* — stand for the first letters of the phrase *Nes Gadol Hayah Sham,* which means, "A great miracle happened there."

Etrog (EH-trohg) (H): A citron, or yellow fruit like a lemon, used during Sukkot.

Froy (rhymes with "boy") (Y): The Yiddish word used to address a married woman, similar to "Mrs.," "Ms.," or "Madam."

Groschen (GROW-shen) (Y): In Eastern Europe, a groschen was the smallest denomination of coin, similar to a penny.

Haggadah (hah-GAH-dah) (H): Literally "to tell." A book discussing the story of Exodus, which is read at the Passover Seder.

Hamantaschen (HAH-men-tah-shen) (Y): Literally "Haman's ears." The three-cornered cookies, filled with fruit or poppyseeds, that are the traditional Purim sweets of Eastern European Jews.

Hanukkah (HAH-noo-kah) (H): A winter holiday commemorating the rededication of the Temple by the Maccabees.

Kiddush (KIH-desh) (Y): From the Hebrew verb *kadesh,* which means "sanctify." This is a special prayer said over a cup of wine on holy days, such as Shabbat, the first and second nights of Passover, and other ceremonial occasions.

Latke (LAHT-kuh) (Y): A pancake, usually a potato pancake, cooked in oil.

Lulav (LOO-lahv) (H): Branches that are waved during the holiday of Sukkot.

Masoret (mah-SOH-reht) (H): Tradition.

Matzah (MATZ-ah) (H): Flat, thin, unleavened bread, eaten mainly during Passover.

Megillah (meh-GEE-lah) (H): A scroll. During the Jewish year, five scrolls are read aloud in synagogue. Each scroll contains a story or poetry from a section of the Bible, appropriate to each of the holidays. They are: The Book of Esther, The Book of Ruth, Ecclesiastes, Lamentations, and The Song of Songs.

Melamed (meh-LAH-med) (Y): Teacher, from the Hebrew verb *lamed*, which means "teach." Like many other Hebrew words, it became incorporated into the vocabulary of Yiddish. The *melamed*, or Hebrew school teacher, was a well-known figure to many Jewish children in the towns of Eastern Europe.

Menorah (meh-NOH-rah) (H): In the Temple in Jerusalem (and in every synagogue today), a seven-branched menorah symbolized the seven days of Creation. The eight-branched menorah, used during Hanukkah, is also known as a "Hanukkiah," to differentiate it from the original Temple candelabra.

Mitzvot (meetz-VOTE) (H): The plural for "mitzvah" or "sacred commandment." The performance of mitzvot is central to traditional Jewish practice and belief. They include ethical behavior, such as charity, kindness to animals, and visiting the sick. Learning and the study of Torah, and ritual acts such as shaking the lulav on Sukkot, are also mitzvot.

Passover or **Pesach** (PAY-sahkh) (H): The Festival of Freedom; an important holiday commemorating the deliverance of Jews from slavery in Egypt.

Purim (POO-rim) (H): A joyous holiday in which the story of Queen Esther is read aloud in synagogue. Costumes, noisemakers, and gifts of food are part of the celebration.

Rosh Hashanah (rosh-hah-shah-NAH) (H): Literally "head of the year," the Jewish New Year.

Safed (SAH-fehd): A small city in central Israel, it became famous in the sixteenth century as a center for Jewish scholars and mystics. Their poetry, philosophy, and ceremonies have enriched Jewish life and observances until the present day.

Seder (SAY-der) (H): The Passover feast.

Shabbat (shah-BAHT) (H): The Sabbath, the seventh day of the week, a day of rest and prayer.

Shalom (shah-LOM) (H): Literally "peace." The traditional Jewish greeting or farewell.

Shofar (show-FAR) (H): Made from a ram's horn, the shofar is one of the most ancient of all Jewish musical instruments, dating back three thousand years. On Rosh Hashanah, each blast of the shofar has its own name, with its own sound and particular meaning. In ancient times, it was also used in battle and to sound alarm.

Sufganiyot (soof-gah-nee-YOT) (H): An Israeli sweet eaten during Hanukkah, similar to American jelly doughnuts.

Sukkah (soo-KAH) (H): A small booth built to celebrate the holiday Sukkot.

Sukkot (soo-COAT) (H): A holiday celebrating the fall harvest.

Synagogue: This is a Greek word meaning "House of Assembly." Perhaps instituted in the sixth century B.C.E., synagogues today serve as the center for Jewish worship, celebrations, and community events all over the world.

Tallit (tah-LEET) (H): A prayer shawl, worn by some Jews during morning prayers every day including Shabbat and holidays.

Tefillin (teh-FILL-in) (H): These are two small, leather boxes containing scriptural passages, which are bound to the left hand and forehead and worn by orthodox Jews during weekday morning services to fulfill an ancient Biblical commandment.

Temple: The Temple referred to in this book is also known as the Second Temple. (The first Temple, built during the reign of King Solomon, was destroyed in 586 B.C.E., which signaled the beginning of the Babylonian exile.) It served as the center of Jewish culture and religion until its destruction in 70 C.E. by the Romans. The Western wall of the Second Temple (also known as the Wailing Wall), which still stands in Jerusalem, is revered as holy ground to the present day.

Torah (toh-RAH) (H): This refers to the Five Books of Moses, which are written by hand on large parchment scrolls and used as the center of synagogue worship. The word *Torah*, however, can also be used to refer to the other books of the Bible or, in some instances, to all of Jewish learning and study.

Yom Kippur (yom-key-POOR) (H): The Day of Atonement. The holiest day of the Jewish year, a day of fasting and contemplation.

BIBLIOGRAPHY

Ausubel, Nathan. *A Treasury of Jewish Folklore.* New York: Crown Publishers, Inc., 1976.

————. *The Book of Jewish Knowledge.* New York: Crown Publishers, Inc., 1971.

Drucker, Malka. *Rosh Ha Shanah and Yom Kippur — Sweet Beginnings.* New York: Holiday House, 1981.

Epstein, Morris. *All About the Jewish Holidays.* New York: Ktav Publishing House Inc., 1970.

Gersh, Harry. *When a Jew Celebrates.* New York: Behrman House, Inc., 1971.

Ginzberg, Louis A. *Legends of the Bible.* Philadelphia: Jewish Publication Society of America, 1956.

Graves, Robert, and Rafael Patai. *Hebrew Myths: The Book of Genesis.* New York: McGraw-Hill Book Co., 1966.

Hautzig, Esther. *The Case Against the Wind and Other Stories by I.L. Peretz.* New York: Macmillan Publishing Co., 1972.

Noy, Dov. *Folktales of Israel.* Chicago: University of Chicago Press, 1963.

Noy, Dov. *Moroccan Jewish Folktales.* New York: Herzl Press, 1966.

Schauss, Hayyim. *A Guide to the Jewish Holy Days.* New York: Schocken Books, 1938.

Schwartz, Howard. *Elijah's Violin and Other Jewish Fairy Tales.* New York: Harper and Row, 1983.

Strassfeld, Michael. *The Jewish Holidays: A Guide and Commentary.* New York: Harper and Row, 1985.

RECOMMENDED TITLES

for further reading on Jewish folklore and the holidays

Goldin, Barbara Diamond. *A Child's Book of Midrash: 52 Stories from the Sages.* New Jersey and London: Jason Aronson, Inc., 1990.

Goodman, Philip. *The Sukkot and Simchat Torah Anthology.* Philadelphia: Jewish Publication Society, 1973.

Howe, Irving, and Eliezer Greenberg. *I.L. Peretz Selected Stories.* New York: Schocken Books, 1975.

Jaffe, Nina. *The Three Riddles: A Jewish Folktale.* New York: Bantam Books, Inc., 1989.

Nahmad, H.M. *A Portion in Paradise and Other Jewish Folktales.* New York: W.W. Norton, 1973.

Schram, Peninnah. *Jewish Stories One Generation Tells Another.* New Jersey and London: Jason Aronson, Inc., 1988.

Schwartz, Howard. *Miriam's Tambourine: Jewish Folktales from Around the World.* New York: MacMillan & Co., 1985.

Waskow, Arthur. *Seasons of Our Joy.* Toronto and New York: Bantam Books, 1982.

Weinreich, Beatrice Silverman. *Yiddish Folktales.* New York: Pantheon Books, Random House, 1988.